GREAT MINDS OF SCIENCE

Leonardo da Vinci

Genius of Art and Science

Jennifer Reed

Enslow Publishers, Inc.

40 Industrial Road   PO Box 38
Box 398   Aldershot
Berkeley Heights, NJ 07922   Hants GU12 6BP
USA   UK

http://www.enslow.com

Library of Congress Cataloging-in-Publication Data

Reed, Jennifer.
    Leonardo da Vinci : genius of art and science / Jennifer Bond Reed.—
1st ed.
      p. cm. — (Great minds of science)
    Includes bibliographical references and index.
    ISBN 0-7660-2500-4
    1. Leonardo, da Vinci, 1452-1519—Juvenile literature. 2. Artists—
Italy—Biography—Juvenile literature. 3. Scientists—Italy—Biography—
Juvenile literature. I. Title. II. Series.
    N6923.L33R38 2005
    709'.2—dc22

                                      2004013401

Printed in the United States of America

10 9 8 7 6 5 4 3 2

To Our Readers:
We have done our best to make sure all Internet addresses in this book were
active and appropriate when we went to press. However, the author and the
publisher have no control over and assume no liability for the material
available on those Internet sites or on other Web sites they may link to. Any
comments or suggestions can be sent by e-mail to comments@enslow.com or
to the address on the back cover.

Illustration Credits: AP/Wide World Photos, pp. 16, 24, 48; Art
Today, Inc., pp. 10, 66, 69, 97, 101; Corel Corporation, pp. 13, 42;
Courtesy of Jeff Reed, p. 6; David Torsiello/ Enslow Publishers, Inc.,
p. 77; Dover Publications, Inc., pp. 8, 31, 35, 54, 57, 62, 80, 86, 89,
92, 108, 114; Enslow Publishers, Inc., pp. 21, 46, 103; J. G. Heck, *The
Complete Encyclopedia of Illustration* (New York: Park Lane, 1979), p. 51.

Cover Illustration: Dover Publications, Inc. (background); AP/Wide
World Photos (inset).

Contents

1 Renaissance Genius   5

2 Young Leonardo   18

3 Art: Queen of Science   27

4 Architect and Engineer   38

5 The Prophet
of Automation   49

6 The Earth and
the Universe   64

7 Leonardo's Polyhedron   74

8 The Human Body   82

9 Other Wonderful Ideas   94

10 A Great Mind Gone   99

Activities   107

Chronology   115

Chapter Notes   117

Glossary   123

Further Reading
and Internet Addresses   126

Index   127

Renaissance Genius

THE MOMENT IS INTENSE. A PILOT IN A twenty-five-ton fighter jet has to locate a tiny aircraft carrier on a huge ocean before it runs out of fuel. Far below in the vast blue sea, the pilot sees the swaying ship bobbing like a tiny buoy. He lowers the retractable landing gear hidden in the belly of the jet. With a huge thud, the jet's wheels hit the floating runway. A hook at the back of the jet grabs a wire to bring the jet to a complete stop. The jet is safe and so is its crew.

The first airplane with retractable landing gear was built in 1930.[1] A retractable landing gear is a gear that can be pulled back under or inside the

An F-18 jet with lowered landing gear about to land upon an aircraft carrier.

airplane. Before and during World War I, airplanes had fixed wheels.[2] The wheels had to stay in place and hung down from the airplane. This caused the plane to fly slower. Without the wheels down, the airplane can fly faster and perform better while in flight.

Before man could fly, he dreamed of soaring to the clouds. One man in particular often dreamed about flight. His name was Leonardo da Vinci. He made sketches showing ways that man could fly. He observed not only birds but bats as well. Leonardo was quick to notice that the feathers on a bird are separated and allow the wind and air to pass through them. He felt this design would make it more difficult to stay in flight compared with a wing made like a bat's wing. "Remember that your flying machine must imitate no other than the bat, because the web is what by its union gives the armour, or strength to the wings."[3]

In his drawing of a flying machine, Leonardo included retractable landing gear. He knew it would make take off and landing safer. Leonardo was a man ahead of his time, and although his flying machine with retractable landing gear was never built in his lifetime, inventors years later would make Leonardo's idea a reality.

Known mostly for his paintings, Leonardo was also interested in studying the sciences. In a life-long quest to find answers to the unknown, Leonardo studied, observed, and wrote about geology, human anatomy, astronomy, optics, and geometry. He was also an architect, engineer, and draftsman. He applied science to everything he observed.

Leonardo kept notebooks and stacks of paper on which he scribbled his ideas and sketches of his inventions. He worked hard on compiling what he learned into books or treatises. He relied on ancient philosophers—Aristotle, Plato, and Socrates—for guidance. He also looked to his contemporaries, including Leon Alberti and Matteo Palmieri, for ideas. But in the end, Leonardo came to his own conclusions. For each subject, whether optics or architecture, Leonardo wrote down his ideas and theories.

A sketch by Leonardo da Vinci of his imagined landing gear.

Today, his ideas and theories have been collected, though much has been lost. Seven thousand pages of Leonardo's notes have been preserved and published. It is believed there once were over fifteen thousand pages. From these manuscripts, scientists, engineers, painters, and writers studying Leonardo da Vinci have learned about one of the greatest minds in history.

When Leonardo da Vinci was born in 1452, Italian Renaissance art was flourishing. His family on his grandmother's side were potters and were well-known in the area. Although his family was well off, he related more to the peasant way of life. Leonardo had little formal education in his early years. He was much happier learning through experience than by reading a book. He learned how the earth worked by observing. He watched how water flowed, how the stars and moon moved in the night sky, and of course, how birds and bats flew.

The human body also fascinated Leonardo. At that time little was known about the human

One of da Vinci's most famous paintings is The Last Supper, *above. The painting continues to spark debate today regarding the meaning behind the expressions and positions held by Jesus and the Apostles.*

body. Physicians and scientists studied animals more than human bodies. Dissecting humans after death was not common. However, Leonardo was given the opportunity to view and eventually take part in some dissections of the human body. In all, it is believed he witnessed thirty dissections of men, women, and children at various ages. He became interested in anatomy. His notebooks are filled with sketches of legs, arms, tendons, muscles, hearts, intestines, the human head, and many other body parts. This set of papers is referred to as Leonardo's *Treatise on Anatomy*. A treatise is an argument in writing that includes a discussion of the facts and principles involved.

He felt that in order to paint the human body, an artist should first study it in depth. An artist should know what a skeleton looks like; how the muscles, tendons, and nerves lie in the body; and how the skin covers it all. Leonardo's detailed drawings amazed many people. The sketches of the human anatomy found in his notebooks show a man who spent years studying anatomy. He wrote, "This, my depiction of the human body will be shown to you just as though you had a real man before you."[4]

Leonardo applied other sciences to his art as well. He taught aerial and linear perspective. He also studied light and shade, which included six books on this subject alone, as well as the theory of colors. He observed the importance of perspective to painting. Perspective is the ability to see objects (or paint them) as they really are. When Leonardo painted, he wanted the picture to look as real as it could. In writing about these topics, the human eye and what it observes also became important to his studies and his understanding of the art of painting. This is why his paintings are so detailed and realistic. Studying the human body and other scientific theories allowed Leonardo to become one of the greatest painters in history.

For the people living during the fifteenth and sixteenth centuries, Leonardo's work raised many questions and possibilities for the future. Two great thinkers during the Renaissance were Paolo Toscanelli and Leon Alberti. Toscanelli followed and plotted the paths of numerous comets. Alberti wrote a famous treatise on painting. This treatise placed importance on the technical aspects of painting and the application of scientific principles to art. Alberti influenced Leonardo. Many of Alberti's techniques can be found in Leonardo's own great work, the *Treatise della Pittura*, the Treatise of Painting.

Leonardo did not always take life so seriously. He enjoyed the simple pleasures of family and

Da Vinci's Mona Lisa *is perhaps the most famous portrait ever painted.*

friends. He enjoyed attending parties and the theater. He even made costumes for a play. As a writer, Leonardo enjoyed creating fables, jokes, and stories.

One of Leonardo's biographers, Gaddiano, wrote shortly after Leonardo's death, "He was most eloquent in speech, and played the lyre well. . . . He enjoyed the company of the common people."[5] Paolo Giovio, who lived during the time of Leonardo, said this about him: "His charm of disposition, his [brilliance] and generosity was not less than the beauty of his appearance. His genius for invention was astounding, and he was the arbiter of all questions relating to beauty and elegance, especially in pageantry."[6] Leonardo was loved and respected by many.

Leonardo never stopped questioning the world around him. His biggest goal was to find the truth. He constantly questioned the writings of ancient philosophers. Science up until the time of the Renaissance was mostly theory. This means that philosophers reasoned out explanations for their questions. Little experimentation had been done since the work of Roger Bacon (1214–1292) two centuries earlier. Leonardo, however, not only theorized about the world around him, he tested his theories through experiments.

Leonardo lived during a great period of history, the Renaissance. Inventions such as the printing press changed the world. Ancient books were being reproduced, and more people had access to books. The study of ancient philosophers was renewed. Although Leonardo disagreed with some ancient philosophers, he relied on their theories and ideas to take him to the next step—the truth.

Some people will disagree with calling Leonardo a scientist. To call him one, perhaps a broader definition of the word should be used. *The American Heritage Dictionary of the English Language* gives this definition: "A person having expert knowledge of one or more sciences, especially a natural or physical science."

Leonardo could fit into this definition.

Renaissance genius of the arts and sciences, Leonardo da Vinci.

Michael White, author of *Leonardo: The First Scientist*, says, "Science is exploration, it is questioning, it is the application of imagination, it is analysis. And so, without doubt, Leonardo was a practitioner of science because he fulfills all these criteria."[7]

Young Leonardo

WHEN LEONARDO WAS BORN, THE WORLD was immediately against him. He was born to a woman named Caterina and a man named Ser Piero Fruosino Di Antonio da Vinci. Piero was only twenty-one years old. He was a notary. Not much is known about his mother. Most scholars believe she was a local peasant girl. Unfortunately, his parents were not married. Caterina had Leonardo out of wedlock, which made Leonardo an illegitimate child. Leonardo's father had no intention of marrying a peasant girl. She was given a home near the da Vinci's so that she could take care of Leonardo. But soon after Leonardo was a year old, she married another man, moved to the other side of town, and started a new family. Leonardo was angry toward his mother for the rest of his life. He felt she had left him.

In fifteenth-century Italy, especially among the middle and lower classes, illegitimate children were disliked by society. They were disadvantaged in life and often not allowed to attend the university. Any hope of becoming a lawyer or doctor was out of the question for Leonardo.[1] He grew up knowing this hard fact of life and it affected the way he saw the world. He himself believed that a child born out of wedlock was mediocre, average. But Leonardo was anything but average.

Leonardo was born in April 1452 near a small town called Vinci, on a Saturday at 10:30 at night. (His traditional birthdate is April 15, but some sources place it on April 24.) His grandfather Antonio recorded it. The da Vinci family had been notaries for many generations.[2] They certified documents, writings, deeds, and contracts. However, Antonio broke away from this tradition and was happy simply owning land. Sometimes he did draw up legal papers and contracts. He recorded Leonardo's birth in a notary notebook.

The name *Vinci* comes from the word for the rushes that grow on the banks of a local stream called the Vincio. They are woven and braided into baskets. Leonardo identified with the intertwined vinci. He often drew pictures of elaborate knots in his notebooks, and he created one to be his emblem, his symbol. Symmetrical knots often appear in his art.[3]

Leonardo's family were well-known land-owners. They lived in the country, where Leonardo was surrounded by a lush landscape that produced olive oil, wine, and flour. Leonardo worked on the land and knew what it meant to get dirty. His uncle had a mill and his half brother was an innkeeper and butcher. He was very close to his uncle, Francesco. In fact, Francesco was more like an older brother to Leonardo than an uncle. Francesco cared for the

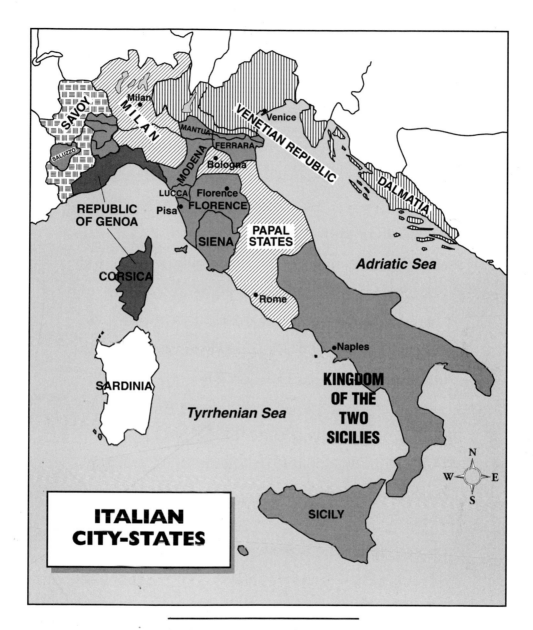

During Leonardo da Vinci's time, Italy was not a whole nation. Instead, it was made up of many smaller city-states, including Venice, Florence, and Rome.

fields and olive groves on his father's farm and taught Leonardo about nature and a love for the land. Leonardo's fascination with nature caused him to think about the earth, the air he breathed, and the water all around him.

Leonardo was in love with learning. It is believed he attended a local school to learn the basics of reading, writing, and arithmetic. He was also taught at home by his eighty-year-old grandfather, Antonio, and Francesco. Much of what he knew he taught himself. Although his illegitimacy helped to train him to learn on his own, it also hurt him terribly.[4]

When Leonardo was just four years old, a hurricane destroyed much of the area where he lived. Ten years later, the Arno River burst its banks and flooded the region. These disasters were the source of Leonardo's obsession with water.[5] He devoted much of his time to the study of water. He wanted to understand it, control it, and find uses for it. Later in his life, he produced many drawings of water as he tried to contain it and put it to good use.

Leonardo had another strike against him besides being illegitimate. He was also left-handed. Like many cultures, Renaissance Italy considered left-handedness abnormal. Parents and teachers would force their left-handed children to write with their right hand.[6] Leonardo never learned to write with his right hand. He used mirror writing, in which he wrote backwards. Most of his writings were written this way. Some historians wonder if he did this to conceal what he was saying or thinking. Some people think he simply wrote this way out of habit. He did use both hands to draw.

Perhaps it was Leonardo's grandmother, Lucia, who encouraged Leonardo in the arts. Her family were potters who produced painted majolica, which is earthenware covered with an opaque (light-blocking) tin glaze and decorated before firing. Some think that Leonardo was acquainted with the art of ceramics and even practiced it.[7]

Soon after the death of Leonardo's grandfather Antonio in 1469, Leonardo moved

*Pictured here is Andrea del Verrocchio's bronze sculpture of David,
with the head of Goliath at his feet. A young Leonardo da Vinci may
have served as del Verrocchio's model for David.*

to Florence to live with his father, Ser Piero. Florence, Italy, was home to a thriving culture. Artisans made their living here. Leonardo was at the age to start an apprenticeship. Boys began an apprenticeship around twelve or thirteen years of age. Although it was recorded that he lived in Vinci with his grandparents until 1468, he visited his father often and likely began learning the arts around 1464 or 1465. His father had friends in the artistic community in Florence, including a well-known sculptor, Andrea del Verrocchio. In 1469, now living with his father, Leonardo became an apprentice for Verrocchio. No art by Leonardo dated before this time has been found.

A Renaissance biographer, Giorgio Vasari, wrote that Leonardo went to work in the workshop of the artist Verrocchio: "He began to practice not only one branch of the arts but all the branches in which design plays a part," even though "he intended to be a painter by profession."[8]

Clearly, Leonardo's childhood played an

enormous role in his adulthood. How he perceived people and objects were all developed by both the good and bad events in his life. Although Leonardo is best known for his paintings, his scientific mind has inspired many. As he created his art, the gears of his mind were always turning.

Constantly learning and always examining and questioning the world around him, Leonardo was an inventor, engineer, scientist, and architect. Even his art was created by applying science and mathematics to the canvas. How do things work? Why does this happen? What if . . . ? Without questions, there are no answers. Leonardo could not live a full life without examining, without discovering. His art, his notebooks, and his ideas still inspire people today.

Art: Queen of Science

FLORENCE WAS THE CENTER OF THE Renaissance in the mid- to late 1400s. In this part of the world, human culture was rapidly developing. Other cities such as Venice, Rome, and even London contributed to the Renaissance, but no city influenced this era more than Florence. Yet only a few people truly contributed to the Renaissance, and they lived relatively short lives. Unfortunately, life expectancy at that time was not long. A man in his thirties would have been considered old. Some of the major figures of the time include Lorenzo de' Medici, sculptor Desiderio da

Settignano, and painter Massaccio. Those who lived in the exciting city of Florence may not have lived long, but they were successful. Leonardo was an exception. He was one of the most successful people of his time, and he lived a long life.

Working in the *bottega* or workshop of Verrocchio was good for Leonardo. Not only did he learn to paint at the workshop, but Verrocchio inspired and encouraged him to be a free thinker. Verrocchio wanted his students to think for themselves and develop their own ideas. Many discussions on science, music, books, and philosophy took place in the workshop. Often, friends of Verrocchio such as Leon Alberti would stop by and talk with the young students.

Once Leonardo became a master, he left Verrocchio's workshop to work on his own. About 1480, while living in Milan, he began his *Treatise on Painting*. This was a lifelong labor of love in which he continued to experiment with different ideas concerning optics (the eye), light and shade, and linear and aerial perspective. Much of his writing is found in notebooks. Originally, Leonardo wanted to combine his notebooks into eight books. These books would cover the scientific aspects of painting, the study of optics, the importance of understanding anatomy, the nature of trees and plants, and the behavior of water. Because painting used many scientific and mathematical elements, Leonardo referred to art as the "queen of science."[1]

During the Renaissance, the works of ancient philosophers were rediscovered. To help him understand optics and the eye, Leonardo turned to these ancient philosophers and their writings. These philosophers included the ancient Greek physician Galen (129–c. 199 A.D.); the Muslim scientists Avicenna (980–1037 A.D.) and Alhazen (965–1040 A.D.), who wrote a treatise titled *A Treasury of Optics*; and the English clerics Roger Bacon (1220–1292) and John Pecham (d. 1292). Contemporaries such as Alberti and Lorenzo Ghiberti also influenced Leonardo's understanding of optics.[2]

Leonardo at first liked what Alberti stated, that vision was light cast between the eye and the object it is looking at. Many scientists thought the eye sent out rays of light toward an object, thus illuminating the object. This theory originated with ancient philosophers and was based on the concept of perspective. Then Leonardo took on the medieval view that the eye received rays of light given off by objects. Medieval philosophers thought that vision took place on a receptive surface of the eye. Finally, after many experiments, Leonardo proposed that the entire eye, not just one part of it, used light, and that it was a complex process. Leonardo often referred to *radiant pyramids* or *visual pyramids* in his writings. He believed that light reached the eye in the form of a pyramid or cone. Alhazen, an Arab physicist known as the father of optics (965–1040), originally theorized about a visual pyramid. Leonardo was no doubt familiar with his work and used Alhazen's findings in his study of the eye.

In one of his many experiments, he

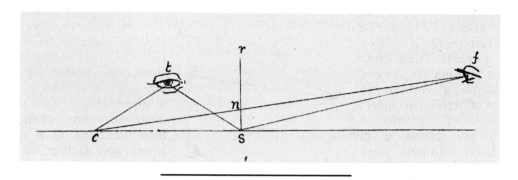

A da Vinci sketch illustrating some of the principles of optics.

demonstrated how the entire pupil receives an image. He did this by holding a needle close to one eye and looking at a distant object. He found that light rays from the distant object are not blocked by the needle and the entire eye receives impulses from all directions and can see the distant object.[3] Therefore, one part of the eye cannot be the only part that receives the light rays.

We now know that light passes through the lens and forms an inverted and backwards image on the retina. This reversed image is then turned around by the brain so that the world is seen right side up. Leonardo worked with mirrors and lenses or glass balls to mimic an eye and its functions. He was possibly the first experimenter to understand the role of the lens. Some people believe that he understood the principle of the contact lens long before its invention. Leonardo wrote that such lenses "would be most useful to the elderly."[4] He dissected eyes, which was extremely difficult. The eyeball would fall apart while he was working. He knew that the eye saw images upside down in what he called the *double inversion process*. He thought the images were again inverted within the eye and not the brain.[5] He wrote many conclusions in his notebook about eyes. Not all were correct, but of course he did not have the technology or understanding that is available today. Some of his correct assumptions include: objects near the eye will appear larger than those at a distance, objects seen with two eyes will appear rounder than if they are seen with only one, a dark object seen against a bright background will appear smaller than it is.[6]

He also discovered that light changes how an

object is seen. For example, he found that the color of one object may be affected by the color of another object and that there is not one true color.

When drawing perspective, Leonardo studied the many different ways a person might view an object. He noted that the perception of the object depended on the line of sight from the eye to the object. In his notebooks, filled with diagrams and explanations, he discusses how the eye can never be a true judge for determining exactly how near one object is to another.

Leonardo's experiments with the eye led to theories on perspective in painting. He studied linear and aerial perspective for a long time. Leonardo writes, "Perspective is the best guide to the art of Painting."[7] Linear perspective is a mathematical system for creating the illusion of space and distance on a flat surface. During the Renaissance, artists wanted their paintings to be as realistic as possible. In order to achieve this, many artists studied perspective.

Although not terribly good at mathematics, Leonardo was good at (and enjoyed) geometry. He wrote in his notebook, "All the problems of perspective are made clear by the five terms of mathematicians, which are: the point, the line, the angle, the superficies [a surface of a body or a region of space] and the solid."[8] To use linear perspective, an artist must first imagine the picture surface as an "open window" through which to see the painted world. Straight lines are then drawn on the canvas to represent the horizon and the "visual rays" connecting the viewer's eye to a point in the distance.[9]

The horizon line is the line that runs across the canvas at eye level. It is also where the land meets the sky in landscape paintings. The vanishing point is the point usually found in the middle of the horizon line. Orthogonal lines are visual rays that help the viewer's eye to connect points around the edges of the canvas to the vanishing point. An artist uses them to line up the edges of straight objects such as walls and paving stones.[10] In *Adoration of the Magi*,

Leonardo carefully drew all of the lines needed to create perspective before sketching in the figures.

Another form of perspective that Leonardo studied in detail was aerial perspective. Aerial perspective creates the feeling of depth in painting by imitating the way the atmosphere makes distant objects appear less distinct and more bluish than they would be if nearby. It is also known as atmospheric perspective. Leonardo says, "There is another kind of perspective which I call Aerial Perspective,

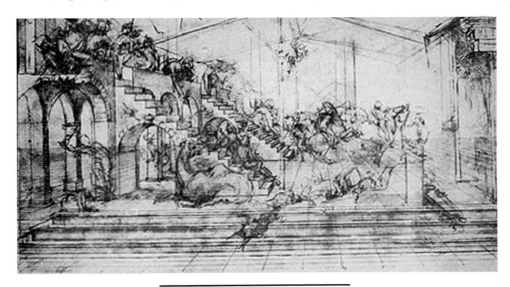

A preliminary sketch of da Vinci's Adoration of the Magi, *showing the artist's use of vanishing point horizon and orthogonal lines.*

because by the atmosphere we are able to distinguish the variations in distance of different buildings."[11] He notes that the atmosphere plays a huge role in how buildings and objects such as mountains appear. Leonardo studied the atmosphere and its colors, which greatly affected aerial perspective in his paintings. He noted that the atmosphere is blue because of the darkness above it and the light below.[12] By mixing colors, Leonardo could recreate the atmosphere in his paintings.

Not only did Leonardo study perspective, he also spent a lot of time studying light, dark, and shadows. "Darkness is the absence of light," he writes. A shadow can never be the same size as the body that casts it. If a body is standing in front of a light, the shadow will always be larger than the body. Why? Leonardo concluded that rays of light begin at a single point. As they are spread in a sphere around this point, radiating through the air, they spread wider.[13]

Leonardo filled pages with diagrams and equations on perspective, optics, light, and shade.

Artists today spend years studying his work and understanding the concepts. Many concepts are taken for granted and are often simple to understand, but Leonardo was the first to study these ideas so intensely, to document them, and to apply them to his own painting. He used science to make him a better painter as well as to understand the world around him. He felt that art was the queen of science because art used so many different aspects of science: optics, mathematics, geometry, perspective, and light.

Architect and Engineer

JUST AS LEONARDO WISHED TO CAPTURE in his writings all of his ideas and theories on the science of art, so too did he wish to record his ideas on architecture and engineering. He filled many pages with sketches of towns, domes, temples, and cathedrals and other buildings. His writing makes up a small volume on the theory of architecture.

Since he was a young man, Leonardo had a fascination for buildings, not just how they appeared to the human eye, but also how they were built. He was greatly influenced by Filippo Brunelleschi, a well-known architect of the time who created the dome for the Florence Cathedral. Leonardo was familiar with Brunelleschi's inventions and mechanical devices and based many of his own ideas on Brunelleschi's. Unfortunately, many of Leonardo's earliest models and architectural drawings have been lost.

The Florence Cathedral dome changed Florence's skyline. Leonardo was twenty years old when it was completed. Its vast scale impressed architects of the time, including Leonardo.[1] In front of the cathedral was a building called The Baptistery, which was in the shape of an octagon. Many architects of the day considered this building to be the best in architectural design. According to historian Giorgio Vasari, Leonardo wanted to make it better by putting steps underneath the church and raising it in a way that would not damage the materials or the church. A man of persuasion, Leonardo convinced some architects that this was a good idea, but the project never happened.

In 1482 Leonardo moved from Florence to Milan. By now he was a master painter. Why he left Florence remains a mystery, but there could be many reasons. Perhaps Florence was not providing this genius of a man with the opportunities to succeed or grow. Once in Milan, the ideal job for Leonardo would have been a court engineer or architect. Hired by the ruler of Milan, Duke Ludovico Sforza, Leonardo could have influence as the court architect. He felt that being an architect was the noblest job a person could have. He sought this position, but it took many years before he found his place in the Milanese court. He did find favor with Sforza and became the court painter. He painted portraits.

Milan and Florence in the late 1400s were similar in many ways. Both were prosperous cities and many well-known and creative people lived there. However, Florence was the home to many painters and sculptors, while Milan was home to musicians, poets, engineers, and scientists. Milan also had one of the best universities in Italy. With access to a well-stocked library, Leonardo spent much of his time reading about mathematics and medicine. He also discussed his ideas with the professors.

The architecture of the two cities was also quite different. Milan was influenced by the architecture of northern Europe. (Only a few beautiful buildings found in Milan were actually designed by Florentine architects, such as Michelozzo and Antonio Filarete.)

Leonardo spent his first years in Milan working on commissions such as the altar piece for the Confraternity of the Immaculate Conception of the Blessed Virgin Mary in the church of San Francesco Grande. The painting was the *Virgin of the Rocks*.

In the summer of 1484 a plague ravaged Milan. Even though sick people were kept apart from the healthy, the disease spread fast. Bodies were piled up in the town square and left until they could be dealt with properly. The plague lasted for nearly two years and killed thousands of people. Leonardo survived the plague, but he

Da Vinci's The Virgin of the Rocks.

wrote little in his notebooks about this time. He did make a sweet-smelling perfume to help cover the stench of death in the city. It is clear, however, that the plague caused him to think about the layout and architecture of cities and towns. He realized that the cramped conditions of Milan allowed disease to spread. He wrote, "If the dwelling is dirty and neglected, the body will be kept by its soul in the same condition, dirty and neglected."[2]

In his sketches for a new city, Leonardo designed houses that were first made in pieces and then assembled on site, much like today's modular homes. He designed roadways that provided plumbing and drainage of water and waste. This idea would house people and animals in a cleaner way: "Let such a city be built near the sea or a large river in order that the dirt of the city may be carried off by the water."[3] There would be areas where people lived and other areas where they worked, as well as neighborhoods for the poor and neighborhoods for the rich.

By the late 1480s Leonardo became involved in the development of the Milan Cathedral. He helped to complete the apse of the cathedral, and he designed a new cupola to replace the old one. Although he was not the main architect, many of his drawings and ideas were used. Leonardo also became friends with a well-known architect named Donato di Angelo, who was known as Bramante. Both men were painters, and both were interested in mathematics and engineering. Bramante's focus however, was architecture. He eventually designed St. Peter's Cathedral in Rome.

Leonardo's notebooks are filled with drawings of cathedrals, towers, spires, arcs, and buildings. He sketched various geometrical shapes. Leonardo enjoyed drawing domes and drew them from different angles. He drew domes rising from a circular base, a square base, and an octagonal base. He created sketches of churches based on the plan of a cross as well as designs that would be best suited for preaching.

Taking architecture one step further,

Leonardo studied the nature of the arch. He was interested in cracks or fissures in walls and why some walls give way and some remain stable. He noted the importance of letting the mortar of a wall dry properly for the correct amount of time; otherwise it would crack.[4] Of course, Leonardo used mathematical equations as well as geometry to reach his conclusions. Leonardo believed that architecture and mathematics were linked. His ability to understand this separates him from other great minds of the Renaissance.

Unlike other engineers of his time, Leonardo wanted to understand how each part of a machine or device worked. He would break down machines and study each piece. One of his earliest known manuscripts, dating to 1478, shows several drawings of mechanical devices. After Leonardo left the studio of Verrocchio, he started thinking about mechanical devices and studying basic mechanical principles. Some of these devices were a winch (a machine that is used for hauling or pulling), a die (a hollow, screw-cutting tool used for forming screw threads), a stamping machine, and a lathe (a machine in which work is rotated on a horizontal axis and shaped by a fixed tool). Leonardo also invented a cranking device for a crossbow.

In the collection of manuscripts called the *Codex Atlanticus*, Leonardo drew pen-and-ink sketches of devices for raising water. He created machines that would bring water from underground and pump water through buildings. He was most fascinated with a mechanism called the Archimedes' screw.

A diagram of Archimedes' screw pump, which is used to raise water.

Leonardo drew a picture of a tower supplied with water from the ground using an Archimedes' screw. Leonardo drew this device as a tightly grooved spiral that allows the water to fall backwards under gravity as the mechanism moves it upward.[5]

Leonardo loved to study screws. He wanted to measure their power and potential in machines. He designed two screw-threading machines. For lifting heavy loads, Leonardo worked with pulleys and pulley blocks. Taking apart the complex pieces of a clock, Leonardo sought to improve how well a clock kept time. He studied cams (a rotating or sliding piece that sends motion to a roller moving against its edge) and pendulums. Leonardo drew beautiful pictures of springs in various shapes and sizes and demonstrated their usefulness in clocks and locks. He even created a spring-making machine.

Leonardo came up with the idea of shock absorbers for his flying machine to cushion the impact if the flying machine crashed. Today, cars and airplanes both use shock absorbers.

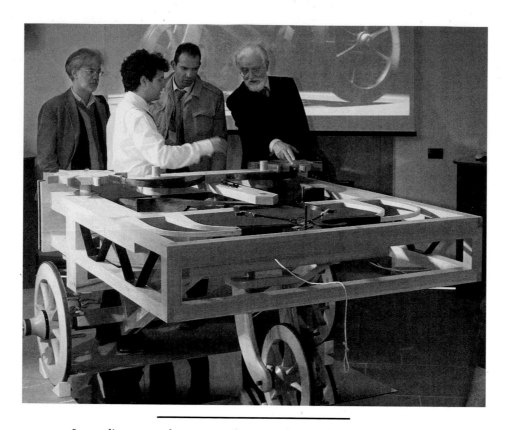

Journalists marvel at a wooden car that was built based on the original designs of Leonardo da Vinci. The car, which operates like a spring-propelled toy, was put on display as part of an exhibition at Florence's Science Museum in April 2004.

Many other ideas of Leonardo's are also a reality today. They include airplanes, submarines, contact lenses, parachutes, scissors, tanks, and the bicycle, to name just a few.

The Prophet
of Automation

WAR WAS ONGOING DURING THE Renaissance and nearly impossible to avoid. Although Leonardo hated war, he also earned money from it by creating weapons and mechanical machines. His mind was full of fantastic ideas.

Leonardo had a fascination for war machines at a young age. In a group of manuscripts dating from 1478, there is a set of illustrations of war machines. Having a love for mechanical devices used in battle as well as out, Leonardo created machines that he hoped would be built and be used.

In 1482 Leonardo hoped he would receive a position in Ludovico Sforza's court. He was made ambassador of the arts and helped Ludovico promote culture in the area, but Leonardo wanted more. He did become a well-known painter in Milan, but Leonardo really wanted a position in the court. He wrote Ludovico a long letter explaining this desire. Of course, he mentioned all the things he could do for the Sforza family. Leonardo wrote that he was an expert in the military arts and knew how to construct bridges and covered ways and that he had methods for destroying any citadel or fortress. He could create secret underground tunnels, covered vehicles, mortars, and other unusual machines of marvelous efficiency. He could also make a bronze horse to glorify the Sforza family.[1]

No one knows if Leonardo sent this letter, but he did receive a commission in 1489 to cast the immense bronze horse. Unfortunately, all the bronze Leonardo had obtained to create this

Da Vinci's design sketches for the Sforza family's bronze horse monument.

monument was used to make cannons when the King of France invaded Italy.

Eventually, Ludovico fell from power and Leonardo returned to Florence, where he became the military engineer and advisor for Cesare Borgia in 1502. Cesare was impressed with Leonardo's vast knowledge. He was also a power-hungry tyrant whom some have compared to Hitler. His motto was, "Caesar or nothing!" Both men were at the height of their careers. Both men were also very different. Leonardo was respected throughout Italy as a master artist. Cesare was a tyrannical ruler. Cesare was a murderer driven by power. Leonardo was a pacifist and vegetarian who did not care about power over others.[2] Some people have questioned why a man like Leonardo would work for such a person. But, Leonardo had to make a living. He was tired of painting and wanted most of all to be an engineer. Now he had his chance.

Leonardo kept a small notebook with him when he traveled with Cesare. It is known today as Manuscript L. In this notebook, he sketched designs for bridges, fortresses, walls, and mechanical devices. It is believed that Leonardo never actually witnessed battle. Rather, he stayed behind dreaming up new ideas. His position with Cesare did not last long. After nine months, Leonardo left his position as military engineer after Cesare killed one of Leonardo's dear friends.

The idea of flight had always captured Leonardo's imagination. It was a lifelong scientific obsession. In 1486 he wrote, "As much pressure is exerted by the object against the air as by the air against the body. And see how the wings, striking against the air, bear up the heavy eagle in the thin air on high."[3]

Many scientists find the first sentence of this record fascinating. It predates Newton's third law by two hundred years! Newton's third law states that for every action (force) in nature there is an equal and opposite reaction. Scientists use this idea when they study aerodynamics. Aerodynamics studies the motion of air and how

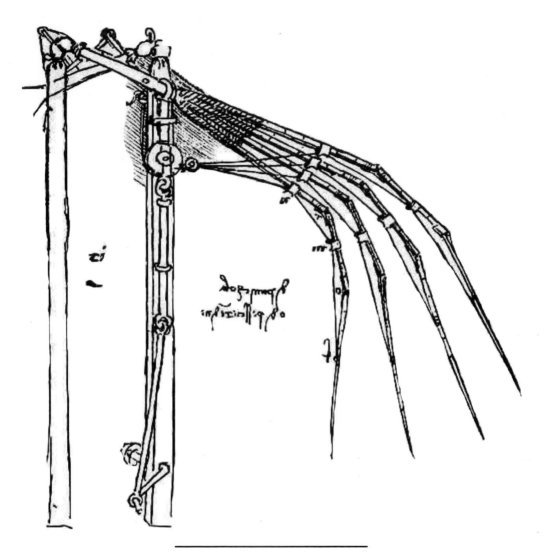

An early da Vinci design of an artificial, bat-like wing.

that motion reacts with objects or bodies in motion. Leonardo realized this much earlier than Newton. The wings of a bird push air downwards. In turn, the air reacts by pushing the bird upwards. This upward force, called *lift*, is what allows the bird to fly.

Although Leonardo did not apply mathematical concepts to this or take it any further, it is clear that Leonardo paid close attention to detail. He studied the bodies of birds and conducted experiments in which he copied specific wing motions. He even re-created the wings of birds and bats: "If you imitate the wings of feathered birds, you will find a much stronger structure, because they are pervious; that is, their feathers are separate and the air passes through them. But the bat is aided by the web that connects the whole and is not pervious."[4]

After much study, Leonardo sketched a flying machine for man. He called his flying machine, "the ship of the air." It had four wings and an operator would stand vertically and move the wings by turning cranks and pressing down on two pedals. Through a mathematical calculation, Leonardo figured out that the man could generate 200 kilograms of power, perhaps enough to get airborne. Unfortunately, technology at the time did not produce enough energy to get man off the ground. Leonardo created a workable flying machine, but only on paper. He never did get off the ground!

Both the flying machine and Leonardo's helicopter are based on sound aerodynamic ideas. He invented a type of helicopter known as the "aerial screw": "I believe that if this screw device is well manufactured, that is, if it is made of linen cloth, the pores of which have been closed with starch, and if the device is promptly reversed, the screw will engage its gear when in the air and it will rise up on high."[5] This idea dates between 1483 and 1486. One idea led to another. Leonardo was well aware of the damage that could occur with his inventions. He knew the need for safety features. He devised ideas for a parachute to be used with the flying machines. He also invented a buoy to keep a person

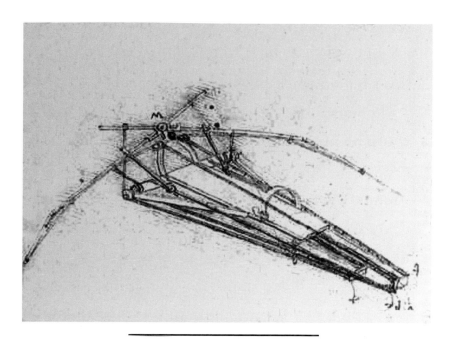

One of Leonardo da Vinci's early designs for a flying machine.

floating if the machine landed in water. Today, many of Leonardo's ideas are used in modern aviation including landing gears, parachutes, life rafts, and inflatable buoys.

Leonardo also conceived of the first armored tank: "I can make covered chariots safe and unattackable, which, entering the enemy with their artillery, there is no body of men so great but they would break them."[6] Leonardo wrote this in his letter to Ludovico Sforza. His tank could be powered either by a horse or by men. Cranks were attached to a trundle wheel, which was then attached to the driving wheels.

Leonardo designed a submersible ship that could be used to sink other ships. Many refer to this as Leonardo's submarine. It was a one-roomed shell big enough for one man. It had a tower on the top with a lid. Leonardo also came up with a way to bring up sunken ships. By attaching air-filled tanks to the hulls, divers could then recover the ships and re-float them.

Although catapults and crossbows were widely used during Leonardo's time, he made them better. The rapid-fire crossbow could fire more arrows in a shorter amount of time, which would cause more damage to the enemy. It was powered by an enormous treadmill. A group of strong men pedaled on steps placed around the rim of a wheel. To protect these men, a large wooden shield was placed behind them. Four crossbows were attached to the wheel, and as it turned, the arrows were released.

Then there was the quick-load catapult. It

had a short firing range. It could be loaded quickly and left loaded for a surprise attack. A man would climb an attached ladder and place the stone in the cup. The arm was bent back with a rope and a winding mechanism. It was released by striking a pin, and then the whole process was repeated. Leonardo also designed missiles to be launched from the catapult. Leonardo was the first to measure the penetrating power of a missile.[7]

Leonardo also designed a breech-loading cannon. A breech-loading cannon is loaded from the back. Previously, muzzle-loading cannons were used. These are cannons that are loaded from the front. He noted that by operating three cannons at one time, the effect would be increased. One would be fired, another loaded, and the third cooling. The cannons during this time had to cool before being reloaded. This wasted time and allowed the enemy to attack. The concept of breech loading was later applied to the machine gun. Some consider Leonardo's device to be the forerunner of today's guns.

Leonardo created recipes for gun powder that would make missiles and bombs that were more effective. He filled shells with gunpowder that exploded on impact and filled a mortar ball with smaller balls. When the large mortar ball split, it sent the smaller balls in different directions. These smaller balls would explode upon impact.

Despite his hatred of war, Leonardo created some impressive war machines. Most were never used. Their beauty does not lie in what each was capable of doing but in how Leonardo used science, mathematics, and even chemistry to create them. He also used his imagination. Where one idea seemed to fail, it would often lead to another.

One of Leonardo's most interesting engineering ideas was a robot. Fascinated with automation, Leonardo was inspired by ancient Greek texts. Hero of Alexandria used several automata in the theater. Arab authors such as Al

Jazari, whom Leonardo also studied, designed complex machines.

Around 1495 Leonardo created the first humanoid robot in Western civilization. His earlier studies on anatomy and kinesiology (the study of the principles of mechanics and anatomy in relation to human movement), contributed to the creation of this robot. When Leonardo was an apprentice at Verrocchio's studio, Verrocchio had designed an automaton clock for the New Marketplace in Florence. No doubt this inspired Leonardo. The robot was more like an armored knight. Leonardo designed it so that it could sit up, wave its arms, and move its head. It could also open and close its jaw as if it were talking or eating. The means of movement and locomotion for robotic devices is called *automata*. Automata devices would later be used in festivals and court masques of the sixteenth and seventeenth centuries.[8]

The robot had two internal systems. The first was the lower half of the robot—the legs, ankles, knees, and hips. The second system moved the

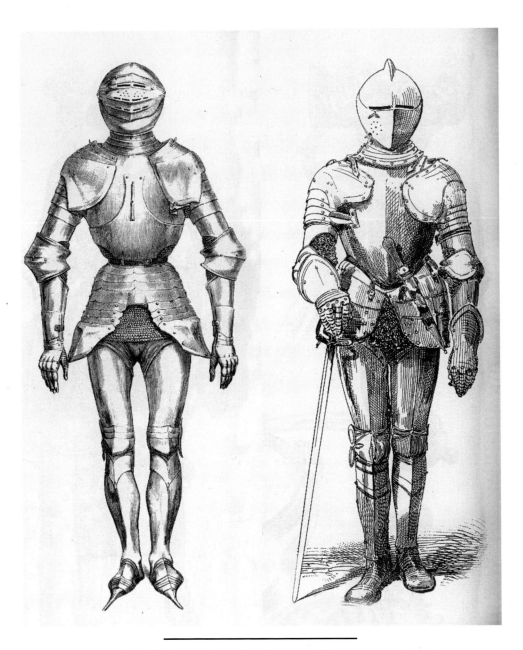

Leonardo da Vinci created a robot that resembled an armored knight, like those pictured above.

arms, shoulders, elbows, wrists, and hands. A mechanical programmable controller (perhaps the first "computer" in Western civilization) within the chest provided the power and control for the arms. The legs were powered by a crank, which drove a cable, which controlled the ankles, knees, and hips.[9]

Today's robots have evolved considerably from Leonardo's first android man. But much of Leonardo's work has been the inspiration for Mark Rosheim's work on anthrobots today. Anthrobotics is creating a robot that moves like a human. The Rosheim 43-axis Robotic Surrogate built for NASA Johnson Space Center is intended to service Space Station Freedom as well as help to colonize Mars.[10] Mark Rosheim, a robotics expert, spent five years piecing together the sketches Leonardo had drawn on numerous pages. Rosheim said, "His anatomy drawings were an inspiration, and I began to see how I could design my own robot, using his first principles."[11]

6

The Earth and the Universe

AS WITH EVERYTHING ELSE AROUND HIM, Leonardo took a great interest in astronomy. Again, he referred to ancient philosophers and quoted them in his notebooks. However, he did not rely heavily on their conclusions. Like many of his day, Leonardo believed that the earth was fixed and that the sun and the moon revolved around it. However, another great scientist of Leonardo's day, Nicolaus Copernicus (1473–1543), believed the planets were heliocentric, meaning they revolve around the sun. He based his theories on geocentric models and mathematical calculations.

The first telescope was invented in 1609 by Galileo Galilei, an Italian scientist. This was nearly ninety years after the death of Leonardo. There was no instrument like a telescope during Leonardo's time, but this did not stop Leonardo from studying objects millions of miles away. Instead, he created an instrument by using a magnifying glass.

Over the years many scientists have disputed whether Leonardo did in fact invent the first telescope. Because of his interest in optical lenses and the use of mirrors, as well as drawings in his notebook, some believe he did invent a telescope. He describes the principles needed to create one: "It is possible to find means by which the eye shall not see remote objects as much diminished as in natural perspective."[1] The moon will be seen larger, Leonardo wrote, and the moon's spots will be better defined. Leonardo stated, "Construct glasses to see the moon magnified."[2] Others argue that Leonardo did not invent the telescope. They think that if he had, he would have used it. It seems his idea

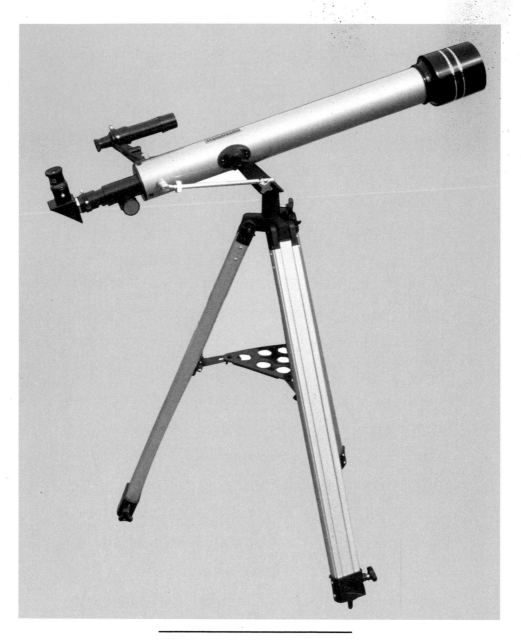

Leonardo da Vinci designed the first telescope. He never actually built a working model, however.

remained on paper and was never actually built and used. Otherwise he would have made observations about the moon, the planets, and the solar system as Galileo did. He could have backed up his theories with proof, if only he could have seen the moon and planets close up.

Still, Leonardo studied the earth and its relation to the sun, moon, stars, and other planets. "The earth is not in the center of the sun's orbit nor at the center of the universe, but in the center of its companion elements, and united with them," he wrote in his notebook.[3] He states that the earth is eccentric to the sun's orbit. *Eccentric* means that it deviates from an established pattern or path. At different times, the earth is not at the center, and so it cannot be the center of the solar system.

Other ideas from Leonardo about the planets and stars are a bit misleading. He noted that the earth is a star.[4] Although not accurate, his reasoning is correct. Leonardo felt that if a person were to stand on the moon or a star, the earth would appear as a bright luminous sphere, just as a person who stands on earth sees the moon and stars as bright luminous spheres. But it is the terms of planet and star, as scientists know them today, that make Leonardo's statement false. Planets and stars are made up of different materials, and stars create their brightness from burning gases. He did suggest that the moon reflects the light from the sun and that it acts like a spherical mirror.[5]

Leonardo also believed that the moon was made from similar materials as the earth. He thought that it was mostly covered in water as well. It is this water, he believed, that reflects the sun's light and makes the moon shine. He notes that some of his peers did not agree with this at all. Also, many of Leonardo's ideas were not his alone but taken from other philosophers, such as Albert of Saxony, who half a century earlier believed that the moon reflected the sun's light.

In addition to the stars and planets, Leonardo also explored the world around him. Although he studied many aspects of the earth, his largest interest lay in the study of water and

Da Vinci developed many theories about the earth, the moon, and other celestial bodies.

how it moved. Leonardo had wanted to create a collection of books dealing solely with water. He went into detail on how these books would be organized. He separated the many characteristics of water: how fresh water is different from salt, how water rises, how it moves through and over objects, how rivers flow, how ocean water moves, and much more.

To Leonardo, water was both terrifying and captivating. He experienced the wrath of water from a hurricane when he was a young boy and knew that water could destroy a civilization. Yet he drew countless pictures of water, rivers, and canals as he tried to capture the energy of water for man's purposes. He drew sketches of deluges, which showed his understanding of the forces of nature and of water.

At this time most people accepted the conclusions of Pliny, a respected ancient authority on the formation of rivers, who believed that rivers came from the ocean. Leonardo disagreed. He followed the idea of another ancient philosopher, Vitruvius, that

Leonardo's Polyhedron

MANY PEOPLE TODAY FIND MATHEMATICS difficult to understand. For Leonardo the same was true. Yet he realized the importance of mathematics as a scientist and an artist. Although his notebooks are filled with geometric figures, calculations, and mathematical symbols, this was one area in which Leonardo did not excel. He knew it, too. Because of his weakness in mathematics, some people today say that he was not a true scientist.

Leonardo purchased a book on mathematics written by Luca Pacioli. It was called *Summa de Arithmetica Geometrica Proportioni et Proportionalita*.

rivers came from the clouds. This is correct; most rivers flow to the ocean, but the source of rivers is rain.

Leonardo also studied the ocean. He observed, "The waters of the salt sea are fresh at the greatest depths."[6] He reasoned that there are freshwater springs below the oceans that send fresh water way up to the surface. Through experiments using a dry linen cloth, one end submerged in salt water and the other submerged in fresh, Leonardo noted that the fresh water rose faster than the salt water. Fresh water was lighter than salt water and so it could rise more easily through the salt water of the ocean. Leonardo's notes on water and the ocean are plentiful. He studied the flow and ebb of the tides, waves and how they break, whirlpools, and even underground water.

Leonardo studied the modern science of hydrodynamics. This is the study of fluids, their motion and how they react to objects. He recognized some of the basic properties of fluids. Today these are called density, viscosity, compressibility, surface tension, and adhesion.

He also wrote about mountains and their relationship to water. In his notebook he wrote, "Mountains are made by the currents of rivers. Mountains are destroyed by the currents of rivers."[7] He studied the Alps and rocks and how a mountain is formed. He studied water erosion. Leonardo recognized the huge role water played in the development of the earth's features.

His book on rain discussed the effect of rain on the environment and how clouds are formed. Leonardo theorized that clouds float at different heights depending on their weight. The weight of a cloud depends on how much moisture it has absorbed. Based on the study, Leonardo invented a hygrometer, an instrument that measures the moisture content of the air and helps predict when it was going to rain.[8] He drew a sketch of a weathervane-like instrument "to know better the direction of the winds."[9]

Leonardo understood that geological changes on the earth happened over a long period of

time. He made a detailed study of fossils three hundred years before their formation was better understood. He concluded that sea shells found at the top of mountains were not put there by a great deluge but by receding oceans. In a study titled *Geological Problems* Leonardo asks many questions about the fossilization of sea shells, how they reached the tops of mountains, and even raises doubt about whether or not the great flood of Noah's time really occurred. "In this work you have first to prove that the shells at a thousand braccia of elevation were not carried there by the deluge, because they are seen to be all at one level, and many mountains are seen be above that level."[10]

It is important to remember that Leo was influenced by ancient philosophers. his ideas stemmed from others and h always the originator of his th Leonardo seemed to have alwa thoughts and ideas of others a st rivers came from the clouds. This is correct; most rivers flow to the ocean, but the source of rivers is rain.

Leonardo also studied the ocean. He observed, "The waters of the salt sea are fresh at the greatest depths."[6] He reasoned that there are freshwater springs below the oceans that send fresh water way up to the surface. Through experiments using a dry linen cloth, one end submerged in salt water and the other submerged in fresh, Leonardo noted that the fresh water rose faster than the salt water. Fresh water was lighter than salt water and so it could rise more easily through the salt water of the ocean. Leonardo's notes on water and the ocean are plentiful. He studied the flow and ebb of the tides, waves and how they break, whirlpools, and even underground water.

Leonardo studied the modern science of hydrodynamics. This is the study of fluids, their motion and how they react to objects. He recognized some of the basic properties of fluids. Today these are called density, viscosity, compressibility, surface tension, and adhesion.

He also wrote about mountains and their relationship to water. In his notebook he wrote, "Mountains are made by the currents of rivers. Mountains are destroyed by the currents of rivers."[7] He studied the Alps and rocks and how a mountain is formed. He studied water erosion. Leonardo recognized the huge role water played in the development of the earth's features.

His book on rain discussed the effect of rain on the environment and how clouds are formed. Leonardo theorized that clouds float at different heights depending on their weight. The weight of a cloud depends on how much moisture it has absorbed. Based on the study, Leonardo invented a hygrometer, an instrument that measures the moisture content of the air and helps predict when it was going to rain.[8] He drew a sketch of a weathervane-like instrument "to know better the direction of the winds."[9]

Leonardo understood that geological changes on the earth happened over a long period of time. He made a detailed study of fossils three hundred years before their formation was better understood. He concluded that sea shells found at the top of mountains were not put there by a great deluge but by receding oceans. In a study titled *Geological Problems* Leonardo asks many questions about the fossilization of sea shells, how they reached the tops of mountains, and even raises doubt about whether or not the great flood of Noah's time really occurred. "In this work you have first to prove that the shells at a thousand braccia of elevation were not carried there by the deluge, because they are seen to be all at one level, and many mountains are seen to be above that level."[10]

It is important to remember that Leonardo was influenced by ancient philosophers. Some of his ideas stemmed from others and he was not always the originator of his theories. But Leonardo seemed to have always taken the thoughts and ideas of others a step further.

Leonardo's Polyhedron

MANY PEOPLE TODAY FIND MATHEMATICS difficult to understand. For Leonardo the same was true. Yet he realized the importance of mathematics as a scientist and an artist. Although his notebooks are filled with geometric figures, calculations, and mathematical symbols, this was one area in which Leonardo did not excel. He knew it, too. Because of his weakness in mathematics, some people today say that he was not a true scientist.

Leonardo purchased a book on mathematics written by Luca Pacioli. It was called *Summa de Arithmetica Geometrica Proportioni et Proportionalita.*

In 1496 he began his studies with Pacioli. Later Luca and Leonardo became good friends. Leonardo knew him for his genius in mathematics while Luca admired Leonardo for his artistic ability, his architecture, and his music. There is no doubt that Leonardo learned a great deal through Luca Pacioli. A few years after their meeting, the two men wrote *De Divina Proportione*, published in Venice in 1509.[1] Leonardo illustrated the book.

Although Leonardo was deficient in some areas of mathematics, he did better in the branch of mathematics called geometry. Geometry deals with the measurements and relationships of points, lines, angles, surfaces, and solids. His notebooks are filled with geometric drawings related to the subjects on which he was working. Whether it was in his architecture, his studies of the eye and light, or his painting, geometrical ideas were everywhere.

The drawings he included in *De Divina Proportione* are remarkable and include the first illustrations of polyhedra ever in the form of "solid edges." A polyhedron is a three-dimensional solid whose faces are polygons joined at their edges. The word *polyhedron* is derived from the Greek *poly* (many) and the Indo-European *hedron* (side). Cubes and pyramids are good examples of polyhedra.

Leonardo's drawings of polyhedra are often "hollow," which allow one to see through the structure to the rear. This was a new form of geometric illustration, and it is believed that Leonardo conceived the idea. In order to draw such an accurate view of polyhedra, Leonardo first created wooden models. From these he created the illustrations.

The arch, a geometrical form, has many variations, and Leonardo studied them all and concluded, "The arch is nothing else than a form originated by two weaknesses, for the arch in buildings is composed of two segments of a circle, each of which being very weak in itself tends to fall."[2] He determined where an arch is weakest, stating that it breaks at the part which lies just below half-way from the center.[3]

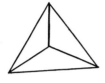 **Tetrahedron: Four faces, all triangles**

 **Cube: Six faces, all squares**

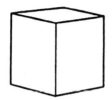 **Octahedron: Eight faces, all triangles**

 **Dodecahedron: Twelve faces, all pentagons**

 **Icosahedron: Twenty faces, all triangles**

The five regular polyhedrons *(polyhedrons possessing faces that are all identical) are illustrated above.*

Leonardo experimented with what would make a strong arch and what would make a weak one. How much weight can an arch hold? What happens in an earthquake and how can an arch survive? Leonardo used his theories and ideas in the architecture of buildings and bridges.

In an experiment he conducted, Leonardo showed that the weight of an object placed on an arch not only pushes down on the columns supporting it, but also pushes outward. To help visualize this, Leonardo wrote that if a man (arch) were in a steel shaft and spread his hands and feet between the walls (columns), the weight of the wall would not lie on the wall itself. The weight will be carried on the shoulders of the man. The more weight put on the man, the harder he will push his hands and feet against the wall. But the weight is carried solely by the man.[4] Leonardo believed that the classic keystone arch could be stretched narrow and widened without losing strength by using a flared foothold, or pier, and the terrain to anchor each end of the span. Leonardo thought of this idea three hundred years before its engineering principles were generally accepted.

Leonardo used geometry to create a bridge. In 1502 Leonardo drew a simple bridge. This bridge was to span 720 feet and go over the Golden Horn, an inlet at the mouth of the Bosphorus River in what is now Turkey. It was a project commissioned by the Sultan Bajazet II of Constantinople (Istanbul).

Leonardo's bridge was not built in his lifetime. In 1996 Norwegian painter and public art creator Vebjørn Sand saw the drawing and a model of the bridge in an exhibition of da Vinci's architectural and engineering designs. The power of the simple design overwhelmed him. He conceived of a project to bring its eternal beauty to life. The Norwegian Leonardo Bridge Project made history as the first of Leonardo's civil engineering designs to be constructed for public use.[5]

The bridge, which is used and admired today, represents a link between the past and present. It expresses the great beauty of Renaissance art

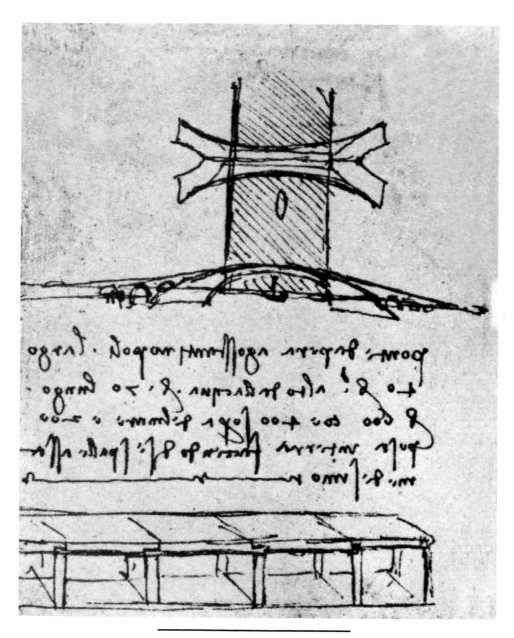

Da Vinci's initial designs for a geometric bridge.

and science, for which Leonardo was best known. The Norwegian Leonardo Bridge was constructed and opened to foot and bicycle traffic on October 31, 2001. Leonardo da Vinci's vision came alive five hundred years after the drawing was made.

8

The Human Body

OFTEN BETTER THAN A PHOTOGRAPH, Leonardo's paintings are famous for their accurate detail. He was able to capture muscle and skin tone, the wave of hair, the figure as it sits or stands—Leonardo was a master at painting the human body. Unfortunately, he did not create many paintings. He spent more time studying the human body than actually painting it. He was interested in the human body from an early age, and it is believed that part of this interest stemmed from his own physical attributes. He was a very handsome man. One biographer, Anonimo Gaddiano, said, "He was a beautiful man, well-proportioned, graceful, and of handsome aspect."[1]

Many painters of the Renaissance studied the human form. They often focused more on the outer physical details of the body—the color and texture of skin and hair, the clothing, the shape of the body. Leonardo was also concerned with these things, but what separates Leonardo from other artists of his time was his desire to know what was inside the body and how it worked. He would be called, among other things, an *anatomist*. An anatomist is a scientist concerned with the internal systems of the human body.

Leonardo's sketches and notes were often better than those of the medical doctors of his time. Dissecting a human body was not widely accepted; it was believed to be immoral. This did not stop Leonardo from witnessing dissections of both humans and animals. Leonardo witnessed up to thirty dissections of men and women of different ages.

During the Renaissance, painters bought their pigments for paints in apothecary shops.

An apothecary shop was a like a pharmacy. Doctors went to apothecary shops to buy materials for their work. Doctors used compounds to create medicines while painters used them to make colorful paints.[2] Often Leonardo would meet physicians there. This may be how he made the contacts that allowed him to view dissections. The conversations Leonardo would have with the doctors may have influenced him as well.

Leonardo first began his anatomical studies in Verrocchio's studio, where he studied the body as an artist would. The depth of study did not go far. As with most artists, Leonardo was concerned more with the outward features of the body. But as time went on, his interest grew more intense, and he studied the human body both inside and out. Leonardo did not formally study the body as if in a university and would not have considered himself an anatomist.[3] But he did pursue this particular interest with a passion.

Leonardo's earliest anatomical drawings date to 1487. His words, "Those hanged of whom I have seen an anatomy," are believed to refer to the hanging death of Bandino Baroncelli, who was hanged after a revolt in 1477.[4] In 1479, Leonardo drew a picture of this hanging, at which he was a spectator.

When Leonardo moved to Milan and began creating the magnificent statue of a horse for the Sforza family, he devoted some time to the dissection of a horse. His drawings depict a horse and its outer physical characteristics, but there are some drawings that compare the muscles of the horse's thigh with those of a man's thigh. This suggests that he was studying the anatomy of both man and horse at the same time.

Based on his earlier drawings, it is believed he had access to various human body parts, including a head, a leg, and a thigh. Still, the lack of dissection material blocked Leonardo's desire to investigate the human body in more detail. It was not until he returned to Florence in the early 1500s that he had a large amount of dissection material available to him. He was then

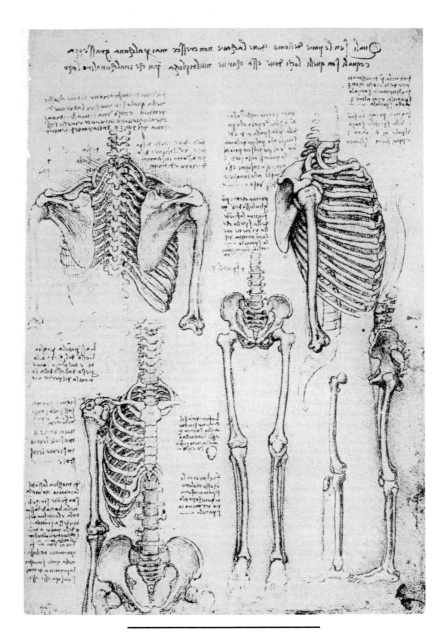

Drawings by da Vinci detailing human skeletal structure.

able to view and dissect bodies at the Hospital of Santa Maria Nuova. Here he met a living hundred-year-old man. Later, when the man died, Leonardo dissected part of his body. Another time, he was able to dissect a two-year-old child.

Leonardo studied the body not only by observing but also through experimentation. For example, he injected wax into the ventricles (small cavities) of the brain in order to learn their shape. It seems he was the first to do such a thing.

As mentioned before, Leonardo studied both animals and humans. Because human bodies were difficult to come by, he often referred to animals. Leonardo was able to partake in some dissections and observe others. His hands-on experiences were limited, but he filled thousands of pages with notes and drawings of his observations.

Osteology is the study of bones. Leonardo drew the skeletal system without having an entire human body to draw from. Around 1489 he acquired a human head, possibly from an execution. He dissected the skull and made a series of illustrations of it. He added to his knowledge of the skeletal system as parts became available. He examined the bones as levers and applied what he knew and understood about mechanics to the movement of the human body. Although there are errors in Leonardo's work, up until his time, illustrations of the skeletal system by other anatomists were poorly done.[5] Leonardo's drawings of bones were superior.

Myology is the study of muscles. It is thought that Leonardo studied muscles so that he could accurately depict the person he was painting. He wanted his paintings to reflect how the muscles move and work together.

Leonardo had no knowledge of blood circulation and did not understand the function of the heart. This frustrated him. Many of his opinions came from other sources. Around 1513, he studied the heart in more detail. However, it was not the human heart Leonardo studied, but that of an ox.[6]

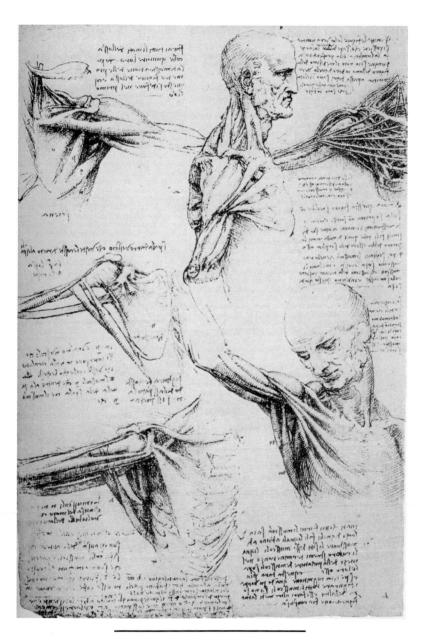

These sketches by da Vinci reflect his understanding of human musculature.

Many of the problems Leonardo had in studying the mystery of innate heat (why our bodies are warm) and blood circulation would only be solved with the discovery of oxygen, which did not occur until much later. His drawings of the heart and valves, although confusing at times, are beyond what had previously been done.

Leonardo concluded that the spinal cord was the center of life.[7] Much of his observation of the nervous system was done on animals. His outstanding contribution to the study of the nervous system was the introduction of an injection technique to obtain casts of the cerebral ventricles (inserting wax into the brain) and his experiments on the nervous system of a frog. Leonardo attempted to understand how the senses worked and, in animals, how they gathered information by their senses.

Leonardo also studied other aspects of the human body, such as the digestive system and the urinary system, and he even studied a seven-month-old fetus. He had wanted to combine his studies into one book called the *Treatise on Anatomy*. Although it never happened, Leonardo did create an outline. His book would start from the time a person was conceived and go through adulthood.

Leonardo drew his famous sketch called the Vitruvian man in 1487. This picture depicts a man with his arms and legs straight out, showing the symmetry and proportions of the human body. Leonardo's drawing is based on the work of an ancient architect Vitruvius, who stated "that the measurements of a man are arranged by Nature thus . . . that is that four fingers make one palm, and four palms make one foot, six palms make one cubit, four cubits make once a man's height, and four cubits make a pace, and twenty-four palms make a man's height, and these measurements are in his buildings."[8]

Leonardo saw this symmetry in architecture, nature, and music, as well as man. "Man is the model of the world," he wrote as he continuously tried to link the structure of the human body to patterns in nature.[9]

Da Vinci's famous "Vitruvian Man" drawing shows the proper proportions of the human figure.

Not everything in Leonardo's notes was accurate or true. Unable to obtain human bodies for study and not knowing certain scientific truths scientists know today, Leonardo was limited in what he could know and understand. However, up until his time, the study of the human body was vague and certainly not well illustrated. Leonardo changed that. The only account of the entire intact collection comes from Cloux, France, where Leonardo was living in 1517. He was visited by Cardinal Louis d'Aragon, and Leonardo showed him his work. Later Cardinal d'Aragon wrote: "[Leonardo] has compiled a special treatise of anatomy with pictorial demonstrations of the limbs as well as of the muscles, nerves, veins, joints, intestines, and whatever can be imagined in the bodies of men as well as women, such as never has been made before by any person."[10] Even to the fellow men of his day, Leonardo was extraordinary.

9

Other Wonderful Ideas

LEONARDO LOVED TO STUDY HOW THINGS moved. He was always looking for ways to make life easier and to use the natural energy of the earth and nature. Some of his ideas would help save lives and improve sanitary conditions. He devised ways to bring water into homes to help clean and sanitize them. Water could also be used in canals and mills to move machinery. He created pumps for an aqualung so a person could swim underwater. Military machinery that resembled today's tanks would protect soldiers from the enemy. Cranes and screws were developed to work inside the automated machineries. His robots and flying machines were all ahead of their time.

This amazing fifteenth-century man created and theorized about many things. Much of what he imagined never came to be and stayed in his notebooks. Other ideas he did see come to life.

In order to make his life easier and wake himself up at a decent hour, Leonardo invented an alarm clock. At that time, engineers were redesigning clocks to keep better time. Clocks were automated and meant to improve people's lives. Leonardo took hundreds of pages of notes on clocks. On paper, he replaced the weights inside clocks with springs, which allowed the clocks to break less and keep better time. From 1495 to 1496 Leonardo used many of the concepts from clocks in creating an automated weaving loom.

His alarm clock was both ingenious and fun. Imagine your feet being lifted quickly into the air while sound asleep. Again, Leonardo used water in his invention. A funnel of water filled up a series of containers. A system of gears and levers would lift the sleeping person's legs and wake him up. "When as much water has been poured through the funnel into the receiver as there is in the opposite balance this balance rises and pours its water into the first receiver; and this being doubled in weight jerks violently upwards the feet of the sleeper, who is thus awakened and goes to his work."[1]

Although it has often been disputed, some people believe Leonardo invented the bicycle. Shortly after Leonardo died, someone pasted his work from the *Codex Atlantis* into a book. Since Leonardo wrote on both sides of the paper, holes were cut out of the blank pages and his notes were pasted in so that both sides could be read. Sometimes though, Leonardo's students also scribbled and drew on the back side of these papers. No holes were cut out for these pages, so the students' work was concealed indefinitely. In the 1970s the book was taken apart in order to better preserve it. On the back of one of the pages were some pictures that students had drawn. This was not unusual except for a small picture of a modern-day bike.[2] The question is, did Leonardo draw this or did one of his students? It is believed, because of the complexity of the bicycle, that Leonardo had drawn it elsewhere and that a student copied it onto this paper.

The bicycle Leonardo created had everything that today's bicycles have. In fact, today's bicycle was created from Leonardo's drawing around

Leonardo da Vinci may have been the first to conceive of the modern-day bicycle.

1885. The concept of unstable two-wheeled motion did not come easily.[3] Leonardo invented this in his head, but it took many years for nineteenth-century engineers to create it.

Even residents of Italy in the fifteenth century wanted to keep cool during hot summer days. Leonardo wanted to improve the lives of people and his invention of the fan was yet another tool devised to do just that! Leonardo's fan compressed air and forced it out of a duct. Although it could be used to keep a room cool, many researchers think that it was probably used to force air into a furnace. The fan could be either water or hand operated.[4]

Leonardo created other automated machines, including a retractable bridge, ladders to scale tall walls, drilling machines, cranes, and more.

10

A Great
Mind Gone

SOME PEOPLE QUESTION WHETHER
Leonardo was a true scientist. Many think he
was. He explored, questioned, analyzed, and
used his imagination to invent machines that
were far beyond his time. He theorized ideas
that would not be understood until hundreds of
years later when technology and science had
advanced. He was a complex man who did not
share much of his own feelings and emotions.
Instead, he focused on creating and finding
answers to the many questions he had about the
world and life in general. What is known about
Leonardo comes partly from his own writings

and partly from the writings of others. From what they say, it is clear that throughout much of his life he was admired and respected by many people.

As much as Leonardo loved science and the mechanics of machines, he also had a passion for the arts. That he loved painting is obvious, but it is also said that he enjoyed entertaining people with his stories. Leonardo was a storyteller. He included in his notebooks fables, prophecies, stories, and humorous writings.

In 1516 Leonardo came to the court of France in Amboise, where he had often been invited. He was far from retiring as he was given the titles "first painter" and "engineer and architect of the king." He created theatrical set pieces, including a mechanical lion to honor the coronation of Francois I. The lion was an automated machine, much like his robot. It walked across the floor, then stopped and opened its chest to reveal flowers.

By this time Leonardo's health was failing. His right arm had become paralyzed. This did

A self portrait by da Vinci, drawn near the end of his life.

not affect him too much since he was left-handed. By now, the printing press was more developed and Leonardo had visions of finally organizing his thousands of pages of notes into books. From 1516 to his death, he did not paint any more masterpieces. He suffered from arthritis, and painting and writing were difficult. Yet it is said that his mind was still sharp.

Leonardo seemed to know that his life was passing and he had little time left. In April of 1519, he made his will. On May 2, 1519, just nine days after he wrote his will he passed away. Leonardo was close to King Francois I and it is said by Vasari, a Leonardo da Vinci biographer, that the king ran to Leonardo's bedside and held him in his arms as he took his last breath.[1]

Leonardo was a man who was always on the move. Not only did he move from place to place several times in his life, but his mind was constantly working. His goal was to find answers about life and ways he could use movement to make life better. His ideas often had a specific use and he worked at creating machines that

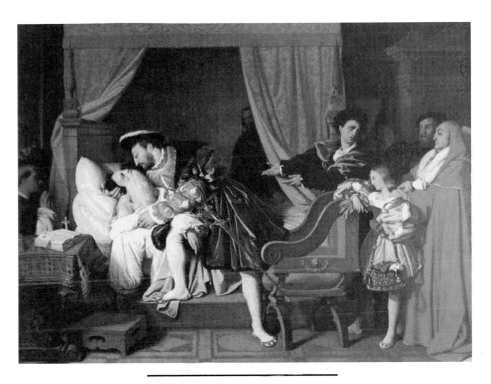

The Death of Leonardo, *painted by Jean Auguste Dominique Ingres in 1818.*

would lighten man's load. If it was not useful, then to Leonardo it was not good. "I would prefer to lose the power of movement than that of usefulness. I would prefer death . . . I never tire of being useful."[2] Leonardo believed that instrumental and mechanical science were the most noble and the most useful of endeavors.[3]

Leonardo was a master artist, an architect, an

engineer, a scientist, and a writer. In all his pursuits, Leonardo applied science. "Science is the captain, and practice the soldiers," he wrote in his notebook.[4] He used many different aspects of science to come up with his theories and then experimented to prove them right. He felt that science was the observation of things possible and there was no such thing as failure. Experience is how Leonardo understood the world. Were all his questions answered when he passed away? Probably not, but he did inspire other great thinkers to continue his legacy to explore, question, and analyze.

Leonardo willed his drawings and notebooks to his faithful disciple, Francesco Melzi. Leonardo met the young boy while living in Milan in 1507. Francesco came to Leonardo when he was young and studied with him until Leonardo's death. They were close friends, and Leonardo trusted only him with his life's work. After Melzi died, he willed his estate to a relative, Orazio Melzi, who had little interest in Leonardo's notes. After many years of hoarding them, Melzi realized what he had and bound the notes into two volumes.

Today, what is left of Leonardo's work is kept in museums and private collections. It has been divided and distributed to those who care about the fate of Leonardo's work. Bill Gates, CEO and founder of Microsoft, purchased the *Codex Leicester* in 1994. It is on display at different museums around the country. Bill Gates had been inspired by Leonardo since he was a young boy. "I've been fascinated by da Vinci's work since I was 10," said Gates. "Leonardo was one of the most amazing people who ever lived. He was a genius in more fields than any scientist of any age, and he was an astonishing painter and sculptor. His notebooks were hundreds of years ahead of their time. They anticipated submarines, helicopters, and other modern inventions."[5]

Mark Elling Rosheim, robotics expert, admits using Leonardo's more primitive robot for inspiration. Today he is creating machines and robotics for NASA. Many painters today use

Leonardo as both a model and for inspiration. Today, he continues to live on in the minds of many as a master artist and scientist. He may have inspired Galileo to make a better telescope to see the stars. Today's philosophers, educators, and scientists all around the world continue to use Leonardo and his great works as examples and inspiration.

Leonardo looked at the smallest things in life and studied them closely to find the answers to his questions. Nothing seems to have escaped his sight. "It should not be hard for you to stop sometimes and look into the stains of walls, or ashes of a fire, or clouds, or mud or like places, in which . . . you may find really marvelous ideas."[6]

Activities

Writing in Reverse

When Leonardo was jotting down his ideas and keeping notes, he often wrote in reverse. He was afraid that other people might steal his ideas and he wanted to make it as difficult as possible for people to read his work. Often it is like a code. Today scholars still find it difficult to read and translate his work.

You will need:

- Paper
- Pencil
- Pens and markers
- Mirror

Refer to the example of Leonardo's signature. Make sure you understand what it means to write backwards. Try writing your name backwards, from right to left. Experiment with writing backward alphabets and backward sentences.

Try this using pens and markers. Is it easier to write backwards using these writing tools? Position a

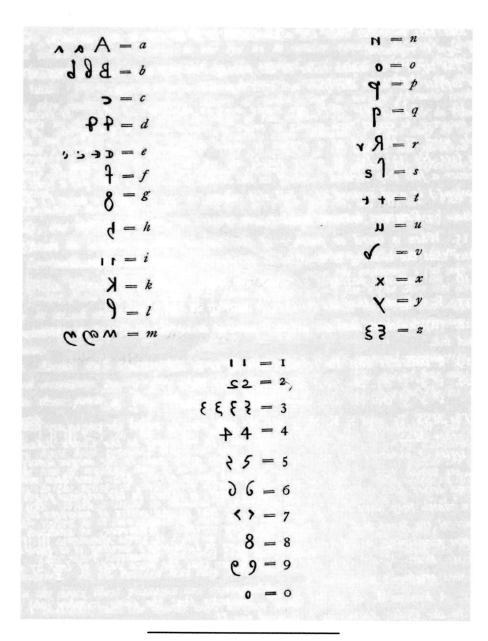

Samples of da Vinci's backward lettering and numbering.

mirror so that the name can be read normally. Write backwards messages to friends.

Are You a Square or Rectangle?

Leonardo was fascinated with the Vitruvian man. Vitruvius, an ancient architect, believed that everything is equally balanced in proportion. Leonardo read Vitruvius's work and applied it to his own painting. This is why Leonardo's depictions of the human body are realistic. They are not only detailed, but also proportionally correct. Leonardo wrote a lot about the proportions of the human figure and used mathematics to figure out the height and width of various parts of the body. He applied these dimensions to his painting and drawings.

How Tall Will You Be?

Leonardo said in his notebook that at the age of three you are half the full height you will grow. If your parents kept records of your growth when you were younger, see if you can find out how tall you were when you were three years old. According to Leonardo, if you were three feet at three years old, then fully grown you would be six feet!

Leonardo believed that in a full grown man, the length of his outspread arms is equal to his height.

You will need:

- A tape measure
- Pencil
- Paper
- People to measure (adults and children)

To find out if you are a square or rectangle, stretch out your arms from each side. Measure the length of your arms from fingertip to fingertip. Write this down on the paper.

Then measure your height from the top of your head to your toes. This is the length of your body. A square has four equal sides. If your width and height are the same, you are a square. A rectangle has two sides that are equal in length and two sides that are equal in width. If your two measurements are different, then you are a rectangle.

If Leonardo's thoughts are correct, then adults should be square. Many children will be rectangles but some will be squares. Because children are constantly growing, their bodies are changing. Depending on where they are in their growth cycle, they can be either squares or rectangles.

Measure a number of adults and children and keep a record of how many are squares and how many are rectangles.

The Sun

An eclipse of the sun occurs when the moon passes between the earth and sun. An eclipse can only occur when there is a full moon. Although it lasts for only a few minutes, it is a special event. But not every eclipse of the sun is a total one. The different kinds of eclipses include total, annular, and hybrid. The next two total solar eclipses will occur on March 29, 2006, and August 1, 2008.[1]

One of Leonardo's many interests was astronomy. He spent many hours looking at the skies. Leonardo experienced many solar eclipses during his lifetime. Only a handful were total eclipses, such as the one in 1485.[2] Still, these amazing astronomical events gave Leonardo a lot to study and think about.

Leonardo referred to the ancients in his notebooks and disagreed openly with their findings about the solar system. He knew that the earth was not the center of the solar system or the universe. Ancient astronomers from Hipparchus on knew that the earth could not be the geometric center of the sun's orbit. Leonardo also disagreed with the idea that the sun was only as big as it looked to the human eye. This thought was first expressed by the ancient philosopher Epicurus, who said that the sun is the size it looks—about a foot across. Leonardo realized, as did other scientists, that this was not the case.

Solar eclipses and lunar eclipses have one thing in common: shadows shaped like cones. Although Leonardo's estimations of the earth's shadow cone were wrong, the techniques he developed to figure out the size of the sun, the moon, and the earth were good.

In a lunar eclipse, if the width of the shadow of the earth is twice the width of the moon, then the width of the earth itself is (very nearly) three times that of the moon—not twice, as one might perhaps think. Archimedes measured the shadow cone as two moon diameters when it is really closer to three.

Leonardo understood celestial depth, which means that the sun, moon, and earth are not the same size at all even though they may look the same size to the human eye. Leonardo knew that the sun was much farther away from the earth than the moon. Although the sun is much larger than the earth and the moon, it looks the same size because it is farther away.

Watching the Sun Eclipse

Leonardo knew that looking at the sun was both painful and harmful to the human eye. The sun is too bright to observe without some kind of protection. How did Leonardo da Vinci watch the sun eclipse without special glasses? He created a method to watch the sun eclipse without hurting his eyes. Although he still viewed the sun with his naked eye, you are strongly advised to never look at the sun directly. Also, never use an optical device, such as binoculars or a telescope, without special "sun filters." Without the filters permanent damage to the eye can occur.

Leonardo wrote in his notebook to take a piece of paper and pierce holes into it with a needle. He thought that a person could observe a solar eclipse through these holes without hurting the eye. Well, Leonardo could very easily have damaged his eye doing this. Most likely he felt that such a small ray of light through the needle hole was not enough to cause serious damage. However, today we know that even the small amount of light penetrating a tiny pin hole can cause serious and permanent damage to the eye.

Using a modification of Leonardo's idea, watching a solar eclipse can be fun and painless.

Materials

- A cardboard tube (a toilet paper or paper towel tube will work okay, but a shipping tube works best)
- A piece of white paper
- Tape
- Needle or pin

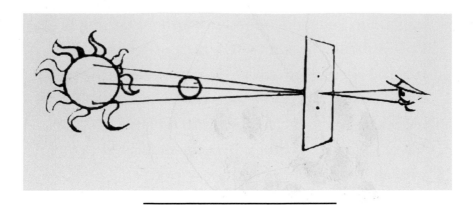

A da Vinci sketch detailing how to properly view an eclipse.

Take the tube and cover both ends with a piece of paper. Tape the paper securely in place. With a needle or pin, puncture one hole in the center of the paper at one end. Hold the end of the tube with a hole up to the sun. At the other end of the tube, you will see an image of the sun. The longer the tube, the larger the image will be. By viewing an eclipse in this way, the eye is protected.

During an eclipse, you can watch the image of the sun move and change. Note, however, that this image is inverted. If the eclipse is happening from the left to the right, the image will show the eclipse occurring from the right to the left. This is a safe way to view the eclipse. This experiment can be done to view the sun at any time. Hold the tube up to the sun and observe the image of the sun during different times of the day.

Chronology

1452—Leonardo da Vinci born near Vinci in Tuscany, Italy, in April. (Traditional date is the 15th.)

1469—Leonardo's grandfather dies at the age of ninety-six.

1472—Becomes a member of the corporation of painters.

1473—Completes first known drawing, *La Valle dell Arno*.

1482—Leonardo goes to Florence, works as an apprentice in the studio of Verrocchio.

1482–1483—Leaves Florence for Milan to join the service of Ludovico Sforza.

1484–1489—Develops interest in the dynamics of flying. Explores human flight. Works on architecture, domes, military engineering, and war machines.

1487–1488—Starts working on anatomical drawings in the manuscripts.

1490—Begins conducting experiments in optics.

1492—Designs a flying machine.

1493—Begins work on the horse statue of Francesco Sforza.

1494—Studies various types of arches.

1495—Paints *The Last Supper*.

1499—The French invade Italy. Leonardo leaves Milan.

1500—Leaves Milan to return to Florence.

1502—Becomes military engineer under Cesare Borgia.

1502–1503—Designs war machines.

1504—Paints the *Mona Lisa*.

1505—Continues studies on the flight of birds. Designs flying machines and tries to square the circle.

1506–1508—Studies fluid elements, water, air, and fire.

1508—Returns to Milan. Continues studying anatomy.

1509—Draws maps of geological surveys of Lombardy and Lake Isea.

1510–1519—Performs detailed anatomical research.

1513—Goes to Rome to seek the patronage of the new Pope, Leo X. Works for Giuliano de Medici in Rome.

1515—The French recapture Milan.

1516—Moves to France to work for Francois I. Right hand is partially paralyzed. Constructs the mechanical lion for the coronation of Francois I, King of France.

1519—Draws up last will and testament on April 23. Dies in Amboise on May 2. Buried in the Church of St. Florentine in Amboise, France.

Chapter Notes

Chapter 1: Renaissance Genius

1. Dwayne A. Day, "Retractable Landing Gear." *U.S. Centennial of Flight Commission.* <http://www.1903to2003.gov/essay/Evolution_of_Technology/landing_gear/Tech16.htm> (December 17, 2003).

2. John H. Lienhard, "No. 926. Retractable Landing Gear," *Engines of Our Ingenuity*, 1988–1997. <http://www.uh.edu/engines/epi926.htm> (December 17, 2003).

3. Jean Paul Richter, *On Flying Machines, Volume II, The Notebooks of Leonardo da Vinci* (New York: Dover, 1970), p. 278.

4. Leonardo da Vinci, *Leonardo on the Human Body* (New York: Dover. 1983), p. 33.

5. Alessandro Vezzosi, *Leonardo da Vinci: The Mind of the Renaissance* (New York: Harry N. Abrams, 1997), p. 130.

6. Ibid., p. 131.

7. Michael White, *Leonardo: The First Scientist* (New York: St. Martins Press, 2000), p. 329.

Chapter 2: Young Leonardo

1. Michael White, *Leonardo: The First Scientist* (New York: St. Martins Press, 2000), p. 15.

2. Alessandro Vezzosi, *Leonardo da Vinci: The Mind of the Renaissance* (New York: Harry N. Abrams, 1997), pp. 14–15.

3. Ibid., p.18.

4. White, p. 26.

5. Ibid., p. 25.

6. Ibid., p. 27.

7. Vezzosi, p. 20.

8. Ibid., p. 25.

Chapter 3: Art: Queen of Science

1. Michael White, *Leonardo: The First Scientist* (New York: St. Martins Press, 2000), p. 55.

2. Alessandro Vezzosi, *Leonardo da Vinci: The Mind of the Renaissance* (New York: Harry N. Abrams, 1997), p. 107.

3. White, p. 313.

4. *Codex Atlanticus*, 83v b.

5. White, p. 315.

6. Jean Paul Richter, *On Flying Machines, Volume II, The Notebooks of Leonardo da Vinci* (New York: Dover, 1970), pp.131, 133.

7. Ibid., p. 27.

8. Ibid., p. 27.

9. *Exploring Linear Perspective*, n.d., <http://www.mos.org/sln/Leonardo/ExploringLinearPerspective.html> (December 17, 2003).

10. Ibid.

11. Richter, p. 159.

12. Ibid., p. 164.

13. Ibid., p. 94.

Chapter 4: Architect and Engineer

    1. Alessandro Vezzosi, *Leonardo da Vinci: The Mind of the Renaissance* (New York: Harry N. Abrams, 1997), p. 33.

    2. Michael White, *Leonardo: The First Scientist* (New York: St. Martins Press, 2000), p. 117.

    3. Jean Paul Richter, *On Flying Machines, Volume II, The Notebooks of Leonardo da Vinci* (New York: Dover, 1970), p. 28.

    4. Ibid., p. 278.

    5. White, p. 90.

Chapter 5: The Prophet of Automation

    1. Alessandro Vezzosi, *Leonardo da Vinci: The Mind of the Renaissance* (New York: Harry N. Abrams, 1997), p. 51.

    2. Michael White, *Leonardo: The First Scientist* (New York: St. Martins Press, 2000), p. 216.

    3. Ibid., p. 300.

    4. Jean Paul Richter, *On Flying Machines, Volume II, The Notebooks of Leonardo da Vinci* (New York: Dover, 1970), p. 278.

    5. *National Museum of Science and Technology*, n.d., <http://www.museoscienza.org/english/leonardo/default.htm> (December 17, 2003).

    6. Richter, p. 397.

    7. "Cannons", *Leonardo: The Man, His Machines*, n.d., <http://www.lairweb.org.nz/leonardo/guns.html> (December 17, 2003).

    8. Mark Elling Rosheim, *Leonardo's Programmable Automaton: A Reconstruction*, n.d., <http://www.anthrobot.com/press/article_leo_programmable.html> (December, 2003).

9. "Leonardo's Robot," *Finmeccanica, Istituto e Museo di Storia della Scienza*, n.d., <http://brunelleschi.imss.fi.it/genscheda.asp?appl=LIR&xsl=slideshow&lingua=ENG&chiave=101791> (July 12, 2004).

10. Ibid.

11. "Space travel enters the 15th Century," *BBC News*, August 13, 1998, <http://news.bbc.co.uk/1/hi/sci/tech/149724.stm> (December 17, 2003).

Chapter 6: The Earth and the Universe

1. Michael White, *Leonardo: The First Scientist* (New York: St. Martins Press, 2000), p. 295.

2. Jean Paul Richter, *On Flying Machines, Volume II, The Notebooks of Leonardo da Vinci* (New York: Dover, 1970), p. 168.

3. Ibid., p. 137.

4. Ibid., p. 139.

5. Ibid., p. 154–155.

6. Ibid., p. 190.

7. Ibid., p. 205.

8. White, p. 288.

9. Richter, p. 220.

10. Ibid., p. 208.

Chapter 7: Leonardo's Polyhedron

1. Michael White, *Leonardo: The First Scientist* (New York: St. Martins Press, 2000), p. 152–153.

2. Jean Paul Richter, *On Flying Machines, Volume II, The Notebooks of Leonardo da Vinci* (New York: Dover, 1970), p. 87.

3. Ibid., p. 86.

4. Ibid., p. 94.

5. *The Leonardo Project*, n.d., <http://www.vebjorn-sand.com/thebridge.htm> (December 6, 2003).

Chapter 8: The Human Body

1. Alessandro Vezzosi, *Leonardo da Vinci: The Mind of the Renaissance* (New York: Harry N. Abrams, 1997), pp.130–131.

2. Jean Paul Richter, *On Flying Machines, Volume II, The Notebooks of Leonardo da Vinci* (New York: Dover, 1970), p. 14.

3. Ibid., p. 18.

4. Ibid., p. 18.

5. Ibid., p. 27.

6. Ibid., p. 29.

7. Ibid., p. 29.

8. Roger Herz-Fischler, "Didactics: Proportions in the Architecture Curriculum," *Nexus Network Journal: Architecture and Mathematics Online*, n.d., <http://www.nexusjournal.com/Didactics-RHF.html> (December 6, 2003).

9. Michael White, *Leonardo: The First Scientist* (New York: St. Martins Press, 2000), p. 166.

10. Ibid., p. 33.

Chapter 9: Other Wonderful Ideas

1. Alessandro Vezzosi, *Leonardo da Vinci: The Mind of the Renaissance* (New York: Harry N. Abrams, 1997), p.144.

2. John H. Leinhard, "No. 888. Leonardo's Bike," *Engines of Our Ingenuity*, n.d., <http://www.uh.edu/admin/engines/epi888.htm> (November 26, 2003).

3. Ibid.

4. "Leonardo," *National Museum of Science and Technology*, n.d., <http://www.museoscienza.org/english/leonardo/ventilatore.htm> (November 26, 2003).

Chapter 10: A Great Mind Gone

1. Alessandro Vezzosi, *Leonardo da Vinci: The Mind of the Renaissance* (New York: Harry N. Abrams, 1997), p. 127.

2. Michael White, *Leonardo: The First Scientist* (New York: St. Martins Press, 2000), p. 198.

3. Jean Paul Richter, *On Flying Machines, Volume II, The Notebooks of Leonardo da Vinci* (New York: Dover, 1970), p. 289.

4. Ibid., p. 290

5. "Bill and Melinda Gates Bringing Leonardo da Vinci's Codex Leicester to Life," *Microsoft.com*, n.d., <http://www.microsoft.com/BillGates/news/codex.asp> (December 2, 2003).

6. Michael White, *Leonardo: The First Scientist* (New York: St. Martins Press, 2000), p. 328.

Activities

1. Fred Espenak, *Solar Eclipses for Beginners*, August 27, 2002, <http://www.mreclipse.com/Special/SEprimer.html> (January 14, 2004).

2. Fred Espenak, "World Atlas of Solar Eclipse Paths: Second Millennium," *NASA/Goddard Space Flight Center*, August 27, 2004, <http://sunearth.gsfc.nasa.gov/eclipse/SEatlas/SEatlas2.html> (January 15, 2004).

Glossary

aerial perspective—Creating a sense of depth in painting by imitating the way the atmosphere makes distant objects appear less distinct. Also known as atmospheric perspective.

annular eclipse—An eclipse in which a thin outer ring of the sun's disk is not covered by the apparently smaller dark disk of the moon.

apothecary—A shopkeeper who prepares and sells drugs or compounds for medicinal purposes.

apprentice—A person who agrees to work for someone else for a period of time in return for training in a trade or art.

apse—A projecting part of a building (such as a church) that is usually semicircular in plan and vaulted.

Archimedes' screw—An ancient device for lifting water. It consists of a spiral tube wrapped around an inclined rod.

battlements—Protective stone railings built along the tops of castle walls, with indentations through which soldiers can shoot while defending the castle.

braccia—A form of measurement to determine length. About the length of the forearm.

cast—To make an object by pouring molten metal into a specially shaped mold and letting it harden.

cupola—A small structure built on top of a roof.

deluge—When water overflows the land.

geography—A science that deals with the earth and life on earth.

horizon line—In perspective this line is drawn across the canvas at the viewer's eye level. It represents the line in nature where the sky appears to meet the ground.

hydrodynamics—A science that deals with the motion of fluids and the forces acting on solid bodies immersed in fluids and in motion.

hygrometer—An instrument used to measure the humidity of the atmosphere.

linear perspective—A mathematical system for creating the illusion of space and distance on a flat surface such as a canvas or wall.

Middle Ages—The period of European history between the last Roman emperor and the Renaissance (476 A.D. to 1453 A.D.).

notary—A public officer who checks the authenticity of various legal documents such as business contracts and deeds for land before giving them an official seal.

orthogonal lines—Straight diagonal lines drawn to connect points around the edges of a picture to the vanishing point. They represent parallel lines receding into the distance and help draw the viewer's eye into the depth of the picture.

patron—A person who supports an artist's work by providing the artist with money and/or food and shelter.

peninsula—A long point of land extending into a body of water.

polyhedron—A polyhedron is a three-dimensional solid whose faces are polygons joined at their edges.

realism—The style of art in which the artist strives to make the painted scene look as real and natural as possible.

Renaissance—The period of Western European history stretching from the early fourteenth century to the mid- to late sixteenth century (early 1300s to mid- to late 1500s). "Renaissance" comes from a French word meaning "rebirth." The term describes the movement that led to new interest and achievement in art, literature, and science.

symbolism—A form of art in which symbols are used to represent ideas.

three dimensional—Having height, width, and depth.

two dimensional—Having height and width only.

vanishing point—The single point in a picture where all parallel lines that run from the viewer to the horizon line appear to come together.

Further Reading

Byrd, Robert. *Leonardo: Beautiful Dreamer*. New York: Dutton, 2003.

Cooper, Margaret. *The Inventions of Leonardo da Vinci*. New York: Macmillan Company, 1967.

Fritz, Jean, and Hudson Talbott. *Leonardo's Horse*. New York. G.P. Putnam's, 2001.

Heinz, Kaehne. *Leonardo da Vinci: Dreams, Schemes and Flying Machines*. New York: Prestel Books, 1999.

Herbert, Janis, and Carol Sabbeth. *Leonardo da Vinci for Kids: His Life and Ideas*. Chicago: Chicago Review Press, 1998.

Romei, Francesca. *Leonardo da Vinci : Artist, Inventor and Scientist of the Renaissance*. Lincoln, Illinois: Peter Bedrick Books, McGraw Hill Publishing, 2001.

Internet Addresses

Exploring Leonardo
http://www.mos.org/sln/Leonardo/LeoHomePage.html

Da Vinci Inventions
http://www.lib.stevens-tech.edu/collections/davinci/inventions/index.html

Museum of Science and Technology: Leonardo
http://www.museoscienza.org/english/leonardo/Default.htm

Index

A

Adoration of the Magi, 34, 35
Al Jazari, 60
alarm clock, 95–96
Albert of Saxony, 68
Alberti, 29–30
Alberti, Leon, 8, 12
Alhazen, 29–30
Archimedes screw, 46–47
Aristotle, 8
armored tank, 57
Avicenna, 29

B

Bacon, Roger, 15, 29
Baroncelli, Bandino, 85
bicycle, 97–98
Borgia, Cesare, 52
Bramante, 44
Brunelleschi, Filippo, 38, 39

C

cannon, 33
  breech-loading, 59
  muzzle-loading, 59
car, 48
Cardinal Louis d'Aragon, 92–93

catapult, 58–59
Codex Atlanticus, 46, 96
Codex Leicester, 105
Copernicus, Nicolaus, 64
crossbow, 58

D

De Divina Proportione, 75
de Medici, Lorenzo, 27
Donato di Angelo, 44

F

fan, 98
Florence cathedral, 39
flying machine, 7, 47, 55, 56, 57
Francois I, 100, 102

G

Gaddiano, 14
Galen, 29
Galileo, 65, 106
Gates, Bill, 105
Geological Problems, 73
geometry, 75, 79
Ghiberti, Lorenzo, 29
Giovio, Paolo, 14
gunpowder, 60

H

human body, 82–93

cardiovascular system, 88
myology, 88
nervous system, 90
osteology, 87
skeleton, 86
hydrodynamics, 71
hygrometer, 72

L

Last Supper, The, 10

M

Manuscript L, 53
Melzi, Francesco, 104
Milan, 40
Milan cathedral, 44
mirror writing, 23, 107–109
Mona Lisa, 13
moon, 67–69

N

Newton, Sir Isaac, 53

O

ocean, 71
optics, 29

P

Pacioli, Luca 74, 75
Palmieri, Matteo, 8
Pecham, John, 29
perspective, 11, 30, 33
aerial perspective, 35–36
linear perspective, 34
plague, 41, 43

Plato, 8
Pliny, 70
polyhedron, 76, 77

R

robot, 61, 63
Rosheim, Mark Elling, 63, 105

S

Sforza, 40, 50–52, 57, 85
bronze horse, 50, 51, 85
Socrates, 8
stars, 67, 68
submarine, 58
sun, 67, 111–114
eclipse of the, 112–114

T

Toscanelli, Paolo 12
Treasury of Optics, 29
Treatise della Pittura, 12
Treatise on Anatomy, 11, 91
Treatise on Painting, 28

V

Vasari, 25, 34, 39
Vebjørn Sand, 79
Verrocchio, 24, 25, 84
Vinci, 19–20, 25
Virgin of the Rocks, 41–42
Vitruvian man, 92
Vitruvius, 70, 91

W

war, 49, 60
White, Michael, 17